MINI
CROCK POT
COOKBOOK

The Ultimate Guide to Effortless Slow Cooking
with Easy & Delicious Recipes for Everyday
Flavorful Adventures

BELL QUINTANA

TABLE OF CONTENT

INTRODUCTION

Hey there! Welcome to our cookbook! Inside, you'll find a bunch of awesome recipes all made for one kitchen hero – your mini crock pot. This book's all about making your life easier and your food tastier. No fuss, no hassle, just delicious meals waiting for you.

Let me break it down for you: we've got everything from breakfast to dinner and even some sweet treats. Think overnight oats, savory soups, hearty mains, and decadent desserts. And guess what? They're all crafted to make your mini crock pot shine!

What's cool about this book is how it's laid out. It's organized into chapters so you can easily flip to what you're craving. Fancy something cozy? Head to the soups section. Need a sweet fix? Go straight to the desserts. It's made to be your kitchen sidekick, helping you cook up amazing dishes without the stress.

Here's the deal: with this book, you're getting simple, tasty recipes that will make your mini crock pot a game-changer in your kitchen. Picture this: flavorful meals bubbling away while you're out doing your thing. When you return, dinner's ready, and it's seriously good. That's what this book's promising – great food without the hassle.

So get ready for a cookbook that's all about making your life easier and your meals way more delicious. Your mini crock pot's about to become your new best friend in the kitchen!

Getting Started: Essential Tips and Techniques

Getting started with mini crock pot cooking is an exciting journey that opens the door to a world of flavors and convenience. Knowing the necessary tips and methods is critical to realising the full potential of these compact culinary workhorses.

1. Choosing the Right Mini Crock Pot:

Selecting the right mini crock pot is the first important step. Consider the appropriate size for your needs, taking in mind the number of servings you intend to prepare. Check that it will fit comfortably in your kitchen and suit your cooking style. Consider programmable settings, temperature control, and easy-to-clean materials.

2. Prepping Ingredients:

Proper preparation is the foundation for excellent mini crock pot cooking. Chop vegetables uniformly to ensure even cooking, as well as trim extra fat from meats to achieve the desired texture. Browning meat before slow cooking can help to bring out the flavours, but it's not always necessary.

3. Layering Ingredients:

Strategically layering ingredients is a technique that can improve your food. Denser, slower-cooking foods, such as root vegetables and meats, go on the bottom, and delicate ingredients, such as herbs and greens, go on top. This ensures that everything cooks evenly and stays together.

4. Liquids and Flavorings:

Slow cooking requires liquid to keep dishes from drying out. To add depth to your dishes, consider utilising broths, sauces, or wine. Remember to season thoroughly at the start of the cooking process, since flavors intensify over time.

5. Mindful Cooking Times:

Each mini crock pot has its own personality, so get to know its cooking hours. While recipes frequently provide basic instructions, it is critical to understand how your unique appliance functions. Some mini crock pots have various heat settings, allowing you to customise cooking times.

6. Avoiding Overfilling:

Refrain from overfilling your crock pot. Allow some room at the top to allow for good heat circulation and to prevent spills. Overfilling might cause inconsistent cooking and a mess in your kitchen.

7. Patience is a Virtue:

Slow and steady is the trademark of mini crock pot cooking. Resist the impulse to often open the lid, as this releases heat and can greatly increase cooking times. Trust the process and let the magic happen as your ingredients combine to create a flavour symphony.

8. Experiment and Adapt:

Mini crock pot cooking is an art form that, like any other, invites experimentation. Feel free to change the recipes to suit your tastes. You'll develop a feel for what works best as you grow more familiar with your little crock pot.

9. Safety First:

While mini crock pots are typically safe equipment, it is critical to follow all safety precautions. To prevent overheating, place your little crock pot on a heat-resistant surface, keep the cable away from the counter edge, and provide adequate ventilation.

10. Cleaning and Maintenance:

The fun of micro crock pot cooking is not only in the preparation but also in the cleanup. Many crock pot components are dishwasher-safe, making cleanup after cooking a breeze. When cleaning and storing your mini crock pot, make sure you follow the manufacturer's directions.

By embracing these important crock pot cooking tips and practices, you will embark on a mini crock pot cooking adventure that will not only simplify your time in the kitchen but will also enrich the flavors of your culinary creations. Enjoy the voyage of exploring the limitless possibilities that mini crock pot cooking has to offer.

CHAPTER 1

Breakfast Delights

With your trusty mini crock pot, explore the lovely world of breakfast creations. These recipes are tailored to transform your mornings into flavorful encounters without the morning rush. Your little crock pot becomes your cooking partner, allowing you to wake up to delicious fragrances and a ready-to-eat breakfast.

1. Overnight Oats Medley

Ingredients:

- 1 cup of rolled oats
- 1 ½ cups of milk (dairy or plant-based)
- 2 tbsp. honey or maple syrup
- ½ teaspoon of vanilla extract
- Pinch of salt
- Toppings for serving: sliced fruits, nuts, seeds, or yoghurt

Instructions:

1. Coat your mini crock pot with nonstick cooking spray or butter.

2. In the crock pot, combine rolled oats, milk, honey or maple syrup, vanilla extract, and a pinch of salt.

3. Stir well to thoroughly blend all ingredients.

4. Cook on low for 6-8 hours, or overnight.

5. Give the oats a thorough stir in the morning. If you want a creamier consistency, add additional milk.

6. Serve in bowls with sliced fruits, nuts, seeds, or a dollop of yoghurt on top.

Tips:

- For extra flavor, experiment with different toppings such as fresh berries, sliced bananas, chopped nuts, or a sprinkling of cinnamon.

- To taste, adjust the sweetness by adding more or less honey/maple syrup.

2. Cinnamon-Apple Quinoa Breakfast

Ingredients:

- One cup of quinoa, rinsed
- 2 cups apple or cider juice
- Two medium peeled, cored, and diced apples
- One tablespoon of cinnamon
- ¼ cup raisins or dried cranberries
- Optional garnish: chopped nuts

Instructions:

1. Combine the quinoa, apple juice or cider, diced apples, cinnamon, and raisins/dried cranberries in your mini crock pot.

2. Stir to thoroughly distribute the ingredients.

3. Cook for 2-3 hours on low, or until the quinoa is cooked and the liquid has been absorbed.

4. Use a fork to fluff the quinoa.

5. Serve in bowls & garnish with chopped nuts if desired.

Tips:

- For a naturally sweet meal, use a sweeter apple variety.

- For a lighter flavour, replace some of the apple juice with water or almond milk.

3. Breakfast Casserole Surprise

Ingredients:

- 6 eggs
- One cup of milk
- 2 cups frozen hash browns
- A cup of cheddar cheese, shredded
- ½ cup diced bell peppers
- Half a cup of diced onions
- Salt & pepper to taste

Instructions:

1. Coat the mini crock pot with cooking spray.

2. In a mixing dish, whisk the eggs, milk, salt, and pepper.

3. In the crock pot, layer frozen hash browns, diced bell peppers, onions, and shredded cheese.

4. Now pour the egg mixture evenly over the layers.

5. Cook for 4-6 hours on low, or until the eggs are set.

6. Serve the breakfast dish in slices straight from the crock pot.

Tips:

- You can customize the casserole by adding cooked bacon, sausage, or your favorite veggies.

- For a neater presentation, allow the casserole to cool slightly before slicing.

4. Peanut Butter-Banana Oatmeal

Ingredients:

- 1 cup of rolled oats
- 2 mashed ripe bananas
- 2 teaspoons peanut butter
- Two (2) cups almond milk (or your preferred milk)
- ½ teaspoon cinnamon
- Optional toppings: sliced bananas, honey drizzle, chopped nuts

Instructions:

1. Lightly grease the mini crock pot.

2. In the crock pot, combine rolled oats, mashed bananas, peanut butter, almond milk, and cinnamon.

3. Mix everything together thoroughly.

4. Cook on low for 2-3 hours, or until the oats are soft.

5. Before serving, thoroughly stir all of the ingredients.

6. If preferred, top with sliced bananas, honey, and chopped almonds.

Tips:

- To control the sweetness, use natural, unsweetened peanut butter.

- If necessary, adjust the consistency by adding more milk.

5. Veggie and Cheese Frittata

Ingredients:

- Six eggs
- ½ cup of milk
- 1 cup spinach, chopped
- ½ cup of diced tomatoes
- ½ cup diced bell peppers
- Half cups of shredded cheddar cheese
- Salt and pepper to taste

Instructions:

1. Grease your mini crock pot.

2. In a bowl, whisk together the eggs, milk, salt, and pepper.

3. In the crock pot, layer spinach, tomatoes, bell peppers, and shredded cheese.

4. Evenly distribute the egg mixture over the layers.

5. Cook for 3-4 hours on low, or until the eggs are set.

6. Finally allow it to cool slightly before slicing.

Tips:

- Add your favorite vegetables or cooked bacon or sausage for added flavour.

- Before serving, use a toothpick or knife to verify if the frittata is fully cooked in the centre.

Enjoy these delectable breakfast recipes, ideal for hectic mornings or lazy brunches, all made in your mini crock pot!

CHAPTER 2

Soups and Stews

Welcome to where your mini crock pot transforms simple ingredients into hearty bowls of delight. From classic chicken noodle soup to hearty beef stews, these recipes provide not only warmth but also a symphony of flavours that simmer to perfection in your trusted kitchen companion.

1. Classic Chicken Noodle Soup

Ingredients:

- Two skinless, boneless chicken breasts
- 4 cups of chicken broth
- Two sliced carrots
- 2 sliced celery stalks
- 1 diced onion

- 2 minced garlic cloves
- 1 tsp. dried thyme
- Salt and pepper to taste
- 2 cups of egg noodles
- Fresh parsley for garnish

Instructions:

1. Place your chicken breasts at the bottom of the mini crock pot.

2. Add chicken broth, carrots, celery, onion, garlic, dried thyme, salt, as well as your pepper.

3. Cook on low for 6-8 hours or high for 3-4 hours, or until the chicken is tender.

4. Remove the chicken, shred it, and return it to the crock pot.

5. Add the egg noodles, cover, and cook on high for another 20-30 minutes, or until the noodles are cooked.

6. Garnish with fresh parsley and serve.

Tips:

- For additional depth, use homemade chicken broth.

- For variety, feel free to add different veggies such as peas or spinach.

2. Beef and Vegetable Stew

Ingredients:

- 1 pound cubed beef stew meat
- 4 cups of beef broth
- Two peeled and diced potatoes
- Two sliced carrots
- One onion, diced
- Two minced garlic cloves
- 1 teaspoon of paprika
- 1 tsp. dried thyme
- Salt & pepper to taste

Instructions:

1. Place the beef stew meat in the mini crock pot.

2. Add in your beef broth, potatoes, carrots, onion, garlic, paprika, dried thyme, salt, & pepper.

3. Cook on low for 6-8 hours or high for 3-4 hours, or until the beef is tender.

4. Taste and adjust seasoning as needed before serving.

5. Serve right away and savour the rich flavours.

Tips:

- Sear the beef cubes before adding them to the crock pot for added richness.

- Experiment with various herbs and spices to create unique flavor profiles.

3. Lentil and Spinach Soup

Ingredients:

- 1 cup rinsed dried lentils
- 4 cups veggie broth
- One (1) diced onion
- 2 sliced carrots
- 2 cut celery stalks
- 2 minced garlic cloves
- 1 teaspoon cumin
- 1 teaspoon smoked paprika
- 2 cups spinach leaves, fresh
- Salt & pepper to taste

Instructions:

1. Combine your lentils, vegetable broth, onion, carrots, celery, garlic, cumin, smoked paprika, salt, & pepper in the mini crock pot.

2. Cover and simmer for 6-8 hours on low or 3-4 hours on high, or until lentils are tender.

3. Add fresh spinach and simmer for another 15-20 minutes, or until wilted.

4. Adjust seasoning if need be & serve hot.

Tips:

- For a touch of acidity, add a small amount of lemon juice or vinegar.

- Because this soup freezes well, it's ideal for meal prep.

4. Butternut Squash Soup

Ingredients:

- 1 medium peeled, seeded, and chopped butternut squash
- 1 peeled, cored, & diced apple
- 1 diced onion
- 3 cups veggie broth
- 1 teaspoon curry powder
- Half teaspoon cinnamon powder
- ¼ teaspoon of ground nutmeg
- Salt and pepper to taste
- Half a cup of coconut milk (optional, for creaminess)

Instructions:

1. In a mini crock pot, combine the butternut squash, apple, onion, vegetable broth, curry powder, cinnamon, nutmeg, salt, and pepper.

2. Cover and simmer for 6-8 hours on low or 3-4 hours on high, or until the squash is soft.

3. Use an immersion blender or your regular blender to puree the soup until smooth.

4. Stir in coconut milk if using and also adjust seasoning if needed.

5. Garnish with a drizzle of coconut milk or a sprinkle of cinnamon and serve hot.

Tips:

- Before adding the chopped butternut squash and apple to the crock pot, bake them in the oven to add depth of flavour.

- Tailor the spices to your personal preferences.

5. Italian Sausage and Kale Soup

Ingredients:

- 1 pound casing-free Italian sausage
- Four cups of chicken broth
- One can of chopped tomatoes (14 oz)
- One (1) diced onion
- Two minced garlic cloves
- Two cups of kale, chopped
- 1 tsp. dried basil

- 1 tablespoon dried oregano
- Salt and pepper to taste
- To serve, grated Parmesan cheese

Instructions:

1. In a skillet over medium heat, brown the Italian sausage, breaking it up into chunks, remove any excess fat as well.

2. Transfer the cooked sausage in a mini crock pot.

3. Add your chicken broth, diced tomatoes (with juice), onion, garlic, dried basil, dried oregano, salt, and pepper.

4. Cook on low for 6-8 hours or high for 3-4 hours, covered.

5. Add chopped kale in the last 30 minutes of cooking time.

6. Garnish with grated Parmesan cheese and serve hot.

Tips:

- Use spicy Italian sausage for an added spice, or a milder variety if desired.

- If desired, replace the kale with spinach or Swiss chard.

Soups and stews are more than simply meals; they're comfort in a bowl. Allow your mini crock pot to do the work while you enjoy the hearty flavours of these healthy meals.

With these recipes, your mini crock pot becomes a vessel for warmth & comfort, offering a variety of soups and stews that will undoubtedly soothe the soul on any chilly day. Enjoy the convenience & flavor of slow-cooked perfection!

CHAPTER 3

Sensational Side Dishes

These Side Dishes, which range from velvety mashed potatoes to caramelised carrots, are intended to offer a delectable touch to your eating experience.

1. Garlic-Herb Mashed Potatoes

Ingredients:

- Two pounds of peeled and chopped potatoes
- Four (4) minced garlic cloves
- ½ cup of chicken or vegetable broth
- ¼ cup butter
- ½ cup milk or cream
- Two teaspoons of fresh herbs, chopped (parsley, thyme, or chives)
- Salt and pepper to taste

Instructions:

1. In the mini crock pot, combine chopped potatoes and minced garlic.

2. Add butter and chicken or veggie broth.

3. Cook for 6-8 hours on low or 3-4 hours on high, or until the potatoes are soft.

4. Now, in the crock pot, mash the potatoes.

5. Until smooth and well blended, stir in milk or cream, fresh herbs, salt, and pepper.

6. Season to taste and keep heated until ready to serve.

Tips:

- For a creamy texture, use Yukon Gold or Russet potatoes.

- For added flavor, top with grated cheese or roasted garlic.

2. Macaroni with Cheese

Ingredients:

- 8 oz. uncooked elbow macaroni
- 2 cups of shredded cheddar cheese
- 1 ½ cups milk

- ½ cup heavy cream
- 2 teaspoons melted butter
- ½ teaspoon mustard powder
- Salt and pepper to taste

Instructions:

1. Cook the elbow macaroni until al dente according to package directions then drain.

2. In your mini crock pot, combine cooked macaroni, shredded cheddar cheese, milk, heavy cream, butter, mustard powder, salt, and pepper.

3. To incorporate all of the ingredients, stir them together.

4. Cook on low for 2-3 hours, or until the cheese melts and the mixture is creamy.

5. To avoid sticking, stir occasionally.

6. Season to taste and serve immediately.

Tips:

- For a spicy kick, sprinkle with paprika or cayenne pepper.

- Before serving, sprinkle breadcrumbs over top for a crunchy texture.

3. Honey-Glazed Carrots

Ingredients:

- 1 pound of baby carrots
- 2 teaspoons melted butter
- 2 teaspoons honey
- 1 tbsp. brown sugar
- ½ teaspoon ground cinnamon
- Salt and pepper to taste
- Chopped fresh parsley for garnish

Instructions:

1. Place your baby carrots in the mini crock pot.

2. Add in the butter, honey, brown sugar, cinnamon, salt, and pepper.

3. Now stir to evenly coat the carrots.

4. Cook on low for 3-4 hours, or until the carrots are soft.

5. Stir every now and again to ensure equal glazing.

6. Before serving, garnish with fresh parsley.

Tips:

- Add a splash of orange juice or orange zest for added richness.

- Adjust the amount of honey or brown sugar to taste.

4. Tangy Lemon-Garlic Broccoli

Ingredients:

- One pound of broccoli florets
- Two tablespoons olive oil
- 2 cloves garlic, minced
- One (1) lemon zest
- Two (2) teaspoons lemon juice
- Salt and pepper to taste
- To serve, grated Parmesan cheese

Instructions:

1. Fill your mini crock pot halfway with broccoli florets.

2. Drizzle with olive oil, then sprinkle with minced garlic, lemon zest, lemon juice, salt, and pepper.

3. Toss to evenly coat the broccoli.

4. Cook for 1-2 hours on low, or until the broccoli is tender-crisp.

5. Serve immediately, topped with grated Parmesan cheese.

Tips:

- To add depth of flavour, roast the broccoli in the oven before placing it in the crock pot.

- For added crunch, garnish with toasted pine nuts or almonds.

5. Balsamic-Glazed Brussels Sprouts

Ingredients:

- One (1) pound trimmed and halved Brussels sprouts
- Two (2) teaspoons of olive oil
- 2 tbsp. balsamic vinegar
- One (1) teaspoon honey
- Two (2) minced garlic cloves
- Salt and pepper to taste
- Toasted pecans (optional) for garnish

Instructions:

1. Firstly, place the Brussels sprouts in the mini crock pot.

2. Drizzle with olive oil, then drizzle with balsamic vinegar, honey, chopped garlic, salt, and pepper.

3. Toss to evenly coat the Brussels sprouts.

4. Cook for 2-3 hours on low, or until the Brussels sprouts are soft.

5. Stir every now and again to ensure even glazing.

6. Serve immediately, topped with toasted pecans if desired.

Tips:

- Adjust the level of sweetness by varying the amount of honey according to taste.

- For a spicy twist, add a sprinkle of red pepper flakes.

These amazing side dishes prepared in your mini crock pot will steal the spotlight at any meal, offering flavors that complement and elevate the main course. Enjoy the ease and pleasure that these recipes bring to your table!

CHAPTER 4

Delicious Main Courses

Welcome to the realm of Delicious Main Courses.
The recipes in this chapter which range from delicate teriyaki chicken to veggie-packed ratatouille, are intended to tantalise your taste buds while also simplifying mealtime.

1. Tender Teriyaki Chicken

Ingredients:

- 4 skinless, boneless chicken breasts
- ½ a cup soy sauce (low sodium)
- ¼ cup of honey
- Two tablespoons rice vinegar
- Two (2) minced garlic cloves
- One teaspoon of grated ginger
- One tablespoon cornstarch
- Toppings: sesame seeds and sliced green onions

Instructions:

1. Firstly, place the chicken breasts in the mini crock pot.

2. Combine soy sauce, honey, rice vinegar, garlic, and ginger in a mixing bowl. Pour this mixture over the chicken.

3. Cook for 4-5 hours on low, or until the chicken is cooked.

4. Remove the chicken at this point and shred it.

5. Make a slurry with cornflour and water in a small bowl. After this, stir into the sauce in the crock pot.

6. Return shredded chicken to the crock pot & stir to coat with the thickened sauce.

7. Serve over rice with sesame seeds and chopped green onions on top.

Tips:

- For some kick of heat, add red pepper flakes or sriracha to the teriyaki sauce.

- For a juicier texture, use chicken thighs instead of breasts.

2. Savory Pot Roast

Ingredients:

- Three (3) beef chuck roast
- One onion (sliced)
- Four peeled and chopped carrots
- Four peeled & diced potatoes
- 2 cups beef stock
- Two (2) tbsp. Worcestershire sauce
- 2 minced garlic cloves
- One teaspoon of dried thyme
- Salt and pepper to taste

Instructions:

1. Place the beef chuck roast in the mini crock pot.

2. Stir in the onion, carrots, and potatoes, as well as the beef broth, Worcestershire sauce, garlic, dried thyme, salt, and pepper.

3. Cook for 8 hours on low, or until the beef is fork-tender.

4. Remove the roast as well as vegetables from the crock pot.

5. Set aside for a few minutes before slicing the roast.

6. Serve the pot roast slices with the cooked vegetables & drizzle with the savory broth.

Tips:

- For additional flavor, sear the beef roast in a hot skillet before adding it in the crock pot.

- To give depth to the dish, add mushrooms or parsnips.

3. Veggie-Packed Ratatouille

Ingredients:

- 1 eggplant, diced
- Two (2) sliced zucchini
- 1 diced bell pepper
- One (1) sliced onion
- Two (2) minced garlic cloves
- 1 can diced tomatoes (14 oz)
- 2 tbsp tomato paste
- 1 tsp. dried basil
- One teaspoon of dried oregano
- Salt and pepper to taste
- Fresh basil for garnish

Instructions:

1. In the mini crock pot, layer chopped eggplant, sliced zucchinis, diced bell pepper, sliced onion, and minced garlic.

2. Pour in the diced tomatoes, tomato paste, dried basil, dried oregano, salt, and pepper over the vegetables.

3.   Gently whisk everything together.

4.   Cook for 6-8 hours on low, or until the vegetables are soft.

5.   Garnish with fresh basil and serve hot.

Tips:

●   Serve over cooked pasta or with crusty bread for a heartier dinner.

●   For a variety of flavours, experiment with extra herbs such as thyme or rosemary.

4. BBQ Pulled Pork

Ingredients:

●   Three (3) pounds pork shoulder or pork butt
●   One (1) chopped onion
●   One (1) cup of barbecue sauce
●   ½ cup apple cider vinegar
●   ¼ cup brown sugar
●   One tablespoon of mustard
●   Two (2) minced garlic cloves
●   One (1) teaspoon smoked paprika
●   Salt and pepper to taste
●   Hamburger rolls or buns for serving

Instructions:

1. Firstly, place sliced onion at the bottom of your mini crock pot.

2. Arrange the pork shoulder over the onions.

3. Combine barbecue sauce, apple cider vinegar, brown sugar, mustard, minced garlic, smoked paprika, salt, and pepper in a mixing bowl. Next, pour it over the pork.

4. Cook for 8 hours on low, or until the pork is fork-tender.

5. Remove the pork from the crock pot and shred it with two forks.

6. Return the shredded pork to the crock pot and mix thoroughly with the sauce.

7. Place the BBQ pulled pork on hamburger buns or rolls and serve.

Tips:

- Vary the amount of brown sugar and apple cider vinegar to adjust the sweetness and tanginess of the sauce.

- You can add a dash of hot sauce for a spicier version.

5. Lemon-Garlic Herb Chicken

Ingredients:

- 4 boneless, skinless chicken thighs
- ½ cup chicken broth
- Juice and zest of 1 lemon
- 4 cloves garlic, minced
- Two teaspoons of olive oil
- 1 tsp. dried thyme
- 1 teaspoon dried rosemary
- Salt and pepper to taste
- Chopped fresh parsley for garnish

Instructions:

1. Firstly, place chicken thighs in your mini crock pot.

2. Combine chicken broth, lemon juice, lemon zest, minced garlic, olive oil, dried thyme, dried rosemary, salt, and pepper in a mixing dish.

3. Pour the above mixture over your chicken thighs.

4. Cook for 4-5 hours on low, or until the chicken is cooked through.

5. Before serving, sprinkle with chopped fresh parsley.

Tips:

- Broil the chicken thighs in the oven for a few minutes after slow cooking to get a crispy skin.

- For added flavor and color, add sliced onions or bell peppers.

These main course recipes prepared in your mini crock pot are sure to impress, offering a wide variety of flavors and textures that cater to every palate. Enjoy the convenience and delectability that these recipes bring to your meal!

CHAPTER 5

Sweet Treats

Discover the world of Sweet Treats, where your mini crock pot produces delightful treats with little effort. These dishes will fulfil your sweet need while also wow your taste buds.

1. Decadent Chocolate Lava Cake

Ingredients:

- ½ cup all-purpose flour
- 1/3 pound cocoa powder
- ½ cup of granulated sugar
- One teaspoon baking powder
- A pinch of salt
- ½ cup milk
- 2 tbsp. melted butter
- One teaspoon of vanilla extract
- ½ cup semi-sweet chocolate chips
- Vanilla ice cream for serving

Instructions:

1. Coat the inside of the mini crock pot with cooking spray.

2. Whisk together the flour, cocoa powder, sugar, baking powder, and salt in a mixing dish.

3. Stir in milk, melted butter, and vanilla extract until combined thoroughly.

4. Fold in the chocolate chips & pour the batter into the crock pot.

5. Cook for 2-3 hours on low, until the cake is set around the edges but still gooey in the centre.

6. Serve with a scoop of vanilla ice cream while still warm.

Tips:

● For a rich chocolate flavor, use high-quality cocoa powder.

● For an elegant touch, sprinkle powdered sugar on top.

2. Apple-Cinnamon Bread Pudding

Ingredients:

- 6 cups cubed bread (preferably French bread)
- 2 peeled, cored, and chopped apples
- Four (4) eggs
- Two cups of milk
- ½ cup granulated sugar
- 1 tsp vanilla extract
- 1 teaspoon of ground cinnamon
- ¼ teaspoon of ground nutmeg
- ¼ cup of raisins (optional)
- Caramel sauce for serving

Instructions:

1. Start by greasing your mini crock pot.

2. Place the cubed bread and diced apples in the crock pot.

3. Whisk together the eggs, milk, sugar, vanilla extract, cinnamon, and nutmeg in a mixing bowl.

4. Pour in the egg mixture over the bread and apples, if you're using raisins, add them at this point.

5. Gently press down on the bread to ensure it is entirely soaked in the liquid.

6. Cook on low for 2-3 hours, or until the custard is set.

7. Serve it warm, drizzled with caramel sauce.

Tips:

- For optimal absorption of the custard mixture, use stale bread.

- And for added indulgence, top with whipped cream.

3. Berry Cobbler Surprise

Ingredients:

- Four cups of mixed berries (strawberries, blueberries, raspberries)
- ½ cup granulated sugar
- One (1) tablespoon cornstarch
- 1 cup of regular flour
- ⅓ cup granulated sugar
- One (1) teaspoon baking powder
- Pinch of salt
- ½ cup melted butter
- For serving, vanilla ice cream or whipped cream

Instructions:

1. In a bowl, toss the various berries with sugar and cornstarch until coated.

2. Put in the berry mixture in the mini crock pot.

3. Now in a separate bowl, combine the flour, sugar, baking powder, & salt.

4.   Add the melted butter & stir until the mixture resembles coarse crumbs.

5.   Next, sprinkle the crumb mixture over the berries in the crock pot.

6.   Cook for 2-3 hours on low, until the topping is golden and the berries are bubbly.

7.   Serve with vanilla ice cream or whipped cream while still warm.

Tips:

*   You can add a dash of lemon juice to the berries for a citrusy zing.

*   For a different flavor profile, replace half of the berries with peaches.

4. Creamy Rice Pudding

Ingredients:

*   1 cup white long-grain rice
*   4 cups of milk
*   Half a cup of granulated sugar
*   1 tsp vanilla extract
*   Half a teaspoon of ground cinnamon
*   A pinch of salt
*   Half a cup of raisins (optional)

- Nutmeg powder for garnish

Instructions:

1. Rinse and drain the rice in cool water.

2. Combine rinsed rice, milk, sugar, vanilla extract, cinnamon, and salt in a mini crock pot.

3. Stir well and, if using, add raisins.

4. Cook for 3-4 hours on low, stirring regularly, until the rice is cooked and the stew thickens.

5. Stir vigorously to attain a creamy consistency.

6. You can serve warm or chilled, sprinkled with ground nutmeg.

Tips:

- To taste, adjust the sweetness by adding more or less sugar.

- Instead of ordinary milk, use half-and-half or coconut milk for extra richness.

5. Chocolate Peanut Butter Fondue

Ingredients:

- 1 cup chocolate chips (milk or semi-sweet)
- Half a cup of creamy peanut butter
- ½ cup heavy cream
- Dippers such as assorted fruits, marshmallows, or pretzels

Instructions:

1. In the mini crock pot, combine the chocolate chips, creamy peanut butter, and heavy cream.

2. Cook for 1-1.5 hours, stirring occassionally, over low heat, until the chocolate is melted and the mixture is smooth.

3. Stir well to thoroughly blend all ingredients.

4. Keep the fondue warm in the crock pot until ready to serve.

5. Serve with dipping fruits, marshmallows, or pretzels.

Tips:

- For added flavor, add a splash of vanilla essence.
- If the fondue thickens too much, you can stir in a little more heavy cream to reach desired consistency.

These dessert recipes showcase the versatility of your mini crock pot in generating delectable desserts, with a lovely diversity of flavors and textures. Enjoy!

Enjoying this book?

If you're digging the flavors and convenience of your mini crock pot, you'll love diving into more culinary adventures! Check out our other crock pot cookbooks, each packed with its own unique collection of recipes designed to tantalize your taste buds and simplify your cooking routine.

If you're a dad looking to whip up delicious meals hassle-free, '*The Easy 5-Ingredient Crock Pot Cookbook for Dads*' is your kitchen savior! This cookbook's your go-to guide, featuring simple, no-fuss recipes crafted with five ingredients or less. Perfect for dads juggling a busy schedule but craving tasty home-cooked meals. Get your hands on this book and level up your cooking game with minimal effort.

The Easy 5-Ingredient Crock Pot Cookbook for Dads

Scan the QR code or <u>click **HERE**</u> if you're reading the eBook for instant access!

If you're a teen or you have a teen who is eager to explore the kitchen and create awesome meals, the 'Crock Pot Cookbook for Teens' is the culinary adventure guide! Packed with easy-to-follow recipes tailored for beginners, this cookbook makes cooking fun and stress-free. Whether you're cooking for yourself or impressing friends and family, this book's got your back.

Crock Pot Cookbook for Teens

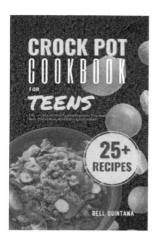 

Scan the QR code or <u>**click HERE**</u> if you're reading the eBook to grab your copy and start your cooking journey today!

If you're navigating the world of solo cooking and craving delicious, fuss-free meals, the '*Crock Pot Cookbook for Singles*' is your kitchen companion! Tailored for those cooking for one, this cookbook serves up recipes that are easy, flavorful, and perfectly portioned. Say goodbye to leftovers and hello to delightful meals designed just for you.

Crock Pot Cookbook for Singles

Scan the QR code or **click HERE** if you're reading the eBook for instant access to your ultimate culinary partner!

CHAPTER 6

Your 14-day Meal Plan

Here's a 14-day meal plan based on the recipes provided in this book.

Day 1:
Breakfast: Overnight Oats Medley
Lunch: Butternut Squash Soup
Dinner: Lemon-Garlic Herb Chicken with Garlic-Herb Mashed Potatoes

Day 2:
Breakfast: Cinnamon-Apple Breakfast Quinoa
Lunch: Italian Sausage and Kale Soup
Dinner: Veggie-Packed Ratatouille

Day 3:
Breakfast: Breakfast Casserole Surprise
Lunch: Lentil and Spinach Soup
Dinner: BBQ Pulled Pork Sandwiches with Balsamic-Glazed Brussels Sprouts

Day 4:
Breakfast: Peanut Butter-Banana Oatmeal
Lunch: Classic Chicken Noodle Soup
Dinner: Savory Pot Roast with Honey-Glazed Carrots

Day 5:
Breakfast: Veggie and Cheese Frittata
Lunch: Butternut Squash Soup
Dinner: Decadent Chocolate Lava Cake (Yes, dessert for dinner today!)

Day 6:
Breakfast: Overnight Oats Medley
Lunch: Lentil and Spinach Soup
Dinner: Tangy Lemon-Garlic Broccoli served with Creamy Mac and Cheese

Day 7:
Breakfast: Cinnamon-Apple Breakfast Quinoa
Lunch: Italian Sausage and Kale Soup
Dinner: Tender Teriyaki Chicken with Garlic-Herb Mashed Potatoes

Day 8:
Breakfast: Breakfast Casserole Surprise
Lunch: Classic Chicken Noodle Soup
Dinner: Veggie-Packed Ratatouille

Day 9:
Breakfast: Peanut Butter-Banana Oatmeal
Lunch: Butternut Squash Soup
Dinner: BBQ Pulled Pork Sandwiches with Balsamic-Glazed Brussels Sprouts

Day 10:
Breakfast: Veggie and Cheese Frittata

Lunch: Lentil and Spinach Soup
Dinner: Savory Pot Roast with Honey-Glazed Carrots

Day 11:
Breakfast: Overnight Oats Medley
Lunch: Italian Sausage and Kale Soup
Dinner: Decadent Chocolate Lava Cake

Day 12:
Breakfast: Cinnamon-Apple Breakfast Quinoa
Lunch: Tangy Lemon-Garlic Broccoli
Dinner: Lemon-Garlic Herb Chicken with Creamy Mac
and Cheese

Day 13:
Breakfast: Breakfast Casserole Surprise
Lunch: Classic Chicken Noodle Soup
Dinner: Veggie-Packed Ratatouille

Day 14:
Breakfast: Peanut Butter-Banana Oatmeal
Lunch: Berry Cobbler Surprise
Dinner: BBQ Pulled Pork Sandwiches with Balsamic-
Glazed Brussels Sprouts

This meal plan provides a diverse range of delicious recipes,
ensuring each day brings a new and delightful culinary
experience!

CONCLUSION

As this culinary journey comes to an end, your mini crock pot has shown to be a kitchen magician, creating delectable and cosy meals with the touch of a button. This selection of dishes has demonstrated the surprising variety and convenience of your compact kitchen companion, from hearty soups simmering with rich flavours to sweet desserts that fulfil the most decadent tastes.

So as you bid adieu to this cookbook, let the aroma of these delicious meals linger in your kitchen, a reminder that culinary delight is always within reach. May the recipes in these pages continue to inspire creativity, stimulate experimentation, and, most importantly, nourish the moments shared at the table.

Here's to many more savoury soups, delicious main dishes, and yummy desserts made possible by the magic of your mini crock pot. Allow its simplicity and ingenuity to inspire you to cook exceptional meals for yourself and your loved ones.

Bon appétit, and happy slow cooking!

Warmest regards,

Bell Quintana

My Little Request

Thank You For Reading This Book!
I really appreciate all of your feedback and
I love to hear what you have to say.

I need your input to make the next version of this
book and my future books better.

Please take two minutes now to leave a helpful review on
Amazon letting me know what you thought of the book:
Thanks so much!
Bell Quintana

NOTES

(For Your Favorite Recipes or Notes)

Attribution

All images used in this book were downloaded from *pixabay.com* and *pexels.com*.

Made in the USA
Las Vegas, NV
04 December 2024

13383077R00037